Fifty Days of Prayer to Invite the Holy Spirit

Acts 29

DR. TERRY TEYKL

Acts 29

Copyright © 1999 Dr. Terry Teykl
Published by Prayer Point Press
Edited by Lynn Ponder

First Edition, 1993
Revised Edition, May 1998
Second Printing, October 1998
Third Printing, October 1999
Fourth Printing, December 2000
Fifth Printing, August 2001

Unless otherwise indicated, all scripture quotations are from the Holy Bible, New International Version © 1973, 1978, 1984 by the International Bible Society. Used by permission of Zondervan Publishing House.

ISBN: 1-57892-045-0
Printed in the United States of America

Prayer Point Press
2100 N. Carrolton Dr.
Muncie, IN 47304
Phone: (765) 759-0215
To order, call toll free: 1 (888) 656-6067

Table of Contents

This book is dedicated to my sister,
Corine Edwards,
who has prayed often and effectively for me.

PREFACE

One of my favorite testimonies that resulted from the original *Acts 29* prayer guide came from a woman who attended the church I used to pastor in College Station, Texas. She was a prayer warrior who quietly and faithfully prayed over our city. She was committed to praying the book of Acts, inviting the Holy Spirit to move in our community just as He had in the early church. She was praying through *Acts 29* with a group of her friends.

Concerned about the activity and influence of a particular bar close to her neighborhood, she began to focus some of her prayer time on the establishment, sometimes even driving around it as she prayed. She believed that if she released the Spirit to work, He would somehow change that bar into a place that could glorify Jesus instead of promoting sin.

I will never forget the look on her face one Sunday when she came to me holding a polaroid picture in her hand of the building that she had been praying over. Not only had the bar shut down, but a new business had taken residence there. The sign on the front now read, "'Praise the Lord' Beauty Salon"!

Acts 29 was first produced five years ago in two parts: a Leader's Guide and a User's Guide. Since then, many churches and individuals have continued to rely on this prayer journey as a tool for meaningful, corporate and personal prayer. The reports have been exciting as churches have invited the Holy Spirit to do the same miraculous things in their midst as He did in the book of Acts. And today, against the backdrop of an ever-increasing global prayer movement, *Acts 29* is more relevant than ever. God is already moving in the earth in a powerful way, and He is waiting for an invitation from you.

This new edition of *Acts 29* has been revised and updated to make it more user friendly and more informative. The Leader's Guide and User's Guide have been combined, giving each individual pray-er a better understanding of the overall objective of praying through the book of Acts. Some of the short lessons have been changed to reflect new ideas while others have remained much the same.

If you are already familiar with *Acts 29*, I hope that you will find this new version to be even richer and more inspirational than the original. If you are new to *Acts 29*, I pray that you will be blessed and challenged as you emerse yourself in the life of the early church and experience the power of the Holy Spirit in your own life.

INTRODUCTION

Several years ago when I was pastoring, one of my church members shared with me something that literally revolutionized my prayer life. It was simple, yet amazingly profound. Not only did it enrich my personal prayer time, but I believe it also impacted our church more than any other program idea.

Mark, who was a college professor, came to me one morning after one of our scheduled times of corporate prayer and told me that he had been claiming the book of Acts for our church. He explained that as he had been studying Acts, reading the testimonies of how the Holy Spirit had moved so dramatically in lives and cities, he was simply asking the Spirit to do the same things in and through our congregation.

I liked it. If we study Acts and preach its wonderful accounts of the works of the Holy Spirit, why not pray it? So I tried it. I picked ten pertinent chapters and started praying them over our church daily. How I was blessed!

I prayed in Acts for two or three months as a part of my

private devotions. Then I asked about thirty people in our church to join me in this experiment for fifty days. They, too, began spending one hour daily praying an outline of the ten chapters I had selected. They were blessed! Next, I added another group to pray the next fifty days. On January 1, 1988, we enlisted 300 people in our church to pray through the book of Acts for fifty days.

> *I could not even begin to recount the things the Holy Spirit did....*

Having been, at that time, a local pastor for twenty-one years, I sensed the need for a fresh move of God. I wanted the Holy Spirit to do the same supernatural works in our lives as He had done in Acts. When I read, "And the Lord added to their number daily those who were being saved" (Acts 2:47), my response was, "Lord, do it again!"

Once we got started, our church was never the same. The presence of the Holy Spirit was undeniable. As we invited Him in, He began to work in individual lives and in the life of our congregation. Our passion for the lost grew; praise and worship became richer; our hunger for the heart of God intensified. And the miracles we saw—I could not even begin to recount the things the Holy Spirit did during that time to draw people to Jesus. In fact, the very same things that happened in the book of Acts began to happen through our church and in our community.

What Makes it so Effective?

Let me share with you five reasons why this prayer journey could be one of the most powerful things your congregation can do as a corporate body.

1. *The Word is a rich and effective prayer language.*

The Word of God is good, and to pray it only makes it better. So often when we pray, we pray the problem instead of the answer. But the Word is the answer, and it is always relevant. It provides us a marvelous language with which we can offer back to God in prayer the truths He has given us. It is creative and expansive, and if we will allow ourselves to be open to the whispers of the Spirit as we pray, He will show us new avenues of intercession through the scriptures.

2. *Praying corporately promotes agreement.*

Jesus said in Matthew 21:13 that His house is to be a "house of prayer." The number one activity in the church should be prayer. In fact, His last command in Luke 24 to the church was to go and form a prayer meeting. He said, "Stay in the city until you have been clothed with power from on high" (Luke 24:49). And then we read in Acts 1:14, "They all joined together constantly in prayer, along with the women and Mary, the mother of Jesus, and his brothers." They were not preaching or teaching or organizing; they were praying just as He instructed them. The early church was birthed in a prayer meeting in the Upper Room. They were "constantly" praying as a unified group.

An extraordinary power force is released when a group of Christians pray together in agreement over a period of time about the same thing. The disciples modeled corporate prayer throughout the book of Acts (Acts 4:23-31, 6:4, 12:5) and I believe this consistent, qualitative, sustained force was the secret of their success.

3. *Praying scripture helps us pray with a kingdom agenda.*

Often our personal prayer agendas range from better jobs to new cars to winning football teams. But Jesus always prayed

His Father's agenda. As you look at His prayer in John 17 you will see no personal request for Himself even though He was facing the cross. His concern pertained to the Father's will and the Kingdom of God.

This prayer plan provides a Kingdom agenda to enable a group of people to pray right on target with what God wants to accomplish in their church and city. It invites people to lay aside their personal agendas and to intercede the scriptural truths of Acts. When we take our eyes off our needs, we have better vision to see how the Kingdom can be advanced in our family, at our workplace and in our community. Furthermore, as we become caught up in praying God's agenda, our needs are often met by the Holy Spirit in the process.

4. Having a prayer plan inspires us to be intentional about prayer.

Sometimes it seems as though we organize everything in the church today except prayer. Consider, for example, the first class organization of the Sunday School program. We recruit and train teachers and we set attendance goals. We invest time and money in providing good curriculum and we keep detailed records for assessing the growth of the program. Or consider the annual pledge campaign which generally has a coordinator, budget, workers and a goal. Nothing is left to chance.

Yet, when it comes to corporate prayer, there is often no list of objectives, no plan, and no one in charge. Its identity is obscured by a maze of other events and programs. I believe when it comes to corporate prayer, we just hope it is going to happen.

Having a corporate prayer plan can help us be just as organized about prayer as we are about any other important ministry in the church. We can budget for materials, assign leaders, recruit and train participants, set goals and assess results. When we aim to involve many people in a visible, organized prayer effort, we are more likely to make the program first class.

5. *As we pray through the book of Acts, we invite the Holy Spirit.*

Prayer plans are helpful, but without the Holy Spirit, they can become programmatic or mechanical just like anything else. But the Bible teaches us that when we pray, the Holy Spirit comes, whether we are aware of it or not. Luke 3:21 says, "When all the people were being baptized, Jesus was baptized too. And as he was praying, heaven was opened and the Holy Spirit descended on him in bodily form like a dove." Later in Luke 11:1-13, Jesus concludes a teaching on prayer by saying, "If you then, though you are evil, know how to give good gifts to your children, how much more will your Father in heaven give the Holy Spirit to those who ask him!"

The presence of the Holy Spirit is crucial to any prayer plan because He is the initiator and teacher of prayer. He takes our techniques, methods, models and plans and makes them fly. Paul says, "In the same way, the Spirit helps us in our weakness. We do not know what we ought to pray, but the Spirit himself intercedes for us with groans that words cannot express" (Romans 8:26). Jesus said of the Holy Spirit, "But the Counselor, the Holy Spirit, whom the Father will send in my name, will teach you all things and will remind you of everything I have said to you" (John 14:26). In 1 John 2:27 Jesus adds, "As for you, the anointing you received from him remains in you, and you do not need anyone to teach you. But as his anointing teaches you about all things and as that anointing is real, not counterfeit—just as it has taught you, remain in him."

So do not be discouraged if your people do not know how to pray at first. Ask the Teacher to teach them the importance and manner of prayer. Even the disciples, who walked with Jesus said to Him, "Lord, teach us to pray" (Luke 11:1).

This prayer guide invites the Holy Spirit to be the initiator and teacher of prayer in our midst, and to invade our community with the awesome love of Jesus Christ in response to our prayers. We are asking Him to work the same miracles now that He did in the book of Acts. To pray these chapters in bold expectation sets us on tip-toe, anticipating what God will do in our midst.

"Acts 29"

As we began to see Acts being rewritten in our own church and city, God impressed something on my heart. Having heard Lloyd Ogilvie coin the phrase "Acts Twenty-Nine" in his book, *Drumbeat of Love*, I realized that the first twenty-eight chapters of Acts, which have no formal closing like other books in the Bible, are not merely stories for us to read and say, "Wow, imagine that!" Instead, they are to be blueprints for us to follow as we write "Acts Twenty-Nine" where we live. The plans go on page after page laying out God's method and manner of ministry in the Spirit. For example, bold preaching yields discernible results; fearless praying catapults the church into areas where it has never been before; radical giving creates an astounding community life.

...many churches are too anemic to affect their cities...

The book is unfinished because the acts of the apostles are not finished. We are His apostles, and the Holy Spirit is still seeking to advance the Kingdom of God in the earth today. But we must be willing to invite Him into our presence.

One of the tragedies I see as I travel around the country is that many churches today are too anemic to affect their cities because they are paralyzed by fear of the Holy Spirit. I call it "pneumophobia." They polish the pews, fine-tune their services, send out visitor letters like clockwork, and busy themselves with spaghetti dinners and ice cream socials. But they resist the Holy Spirit because they are afraid of losing control. They are afraid that if they invite His presence into their services, something different might happen — something that is not in the bulletin!

How sad for a body of believers to be so sealed off in their tidy, religious routines that they miss the new thing God is doing in the world. Revival is *here;* the Spirit is being poured out like never before. People are being healed, and large numbers of unbelievers are coming to Christ. Your church can either batten down the hatches and teeter along in the same, lame and tame, or you can throw open the doors and windows and cry, "Come, Holy Spirit! As you did in the book of Acts, do it again!"

THE HOLY SPIRIT

The Acts of the Apostles could have easily been called the Acts of the Holy Spirit. On every page you can see the Spirit fully at work leading, guiding, teaching, doing the works of Jesus and empowering the church to proclaim the Kingdom of God. In the economy of God, when we pray, we receive the Holy Spirit and He receives us. When we pray, we release Him to work in us and in our church and city. It is this principle that makes prayer so important.

The book of Acts is a testimony to this prayer principle as seen in the lives of the disciples. In Acts 1:14 they prayed, and in Acts 2 the Holy Spirit came upon them. In Acts 4:31 they prayed, and the Evangelist came. In Acts 8:15 "they prayed for them that they might receive the Holy Spirit." The pattern is simple: they prayed, the Holy Spirit came, and they evangelized. And as you know, thousands of people were saved as a result of their preaching. For the disciples, praying was like inhaling the breath of God, and evangelism happened naturally as they exhaled what they had received.

The principles of God never change, because He is the same today as He was the day Peter preached after Pentecost. As you pray through *Acts 29*, you are calling into effect the principle of prayer to be applied to your neighborhood, local high school, church, civic government. Remember in Luke 11, God promises to send the Holy Spirit to those who ask. Obviously, this is not a one time shot of spiritual power when we are converted, but rather the result of a constant asking and seeking for Him to send His Spirit to enable and enliven us (Luke 18:7).

The Holy Spirit is the real Evangelist. Regardless of where or with whom we would like to share Jesus, we must work with the Spirit, through the Spirit and by the Spirit. We are only here to release Him to work. This is the foundation of *Acts 29* — that when we pray, He goes to work in us and in the non-believer to accomplish God's purpose.

The Holy Spirit's Work in Us

1. Compassion

"For God so loved the world He gave His only son" (John 3:16). To have a passion for evangelism is to care enough about the souls of those we meet that we will go to any length to see that they are secured for eternity. We reach out to people because we love, and we love because He first loved us. Love is the driving force. The first thing the Spirit does in us when we begin to pray is to put the compassion of Jesus in our hearts for those outside the church, especially those who are hurting, confused and unlovable.

As the disciples watched Jesus be whipped and crucified, I am sure that the unjust brutality to the one they loved did not inspire in them warm thoughts of friendship or compassion for His executioners. But think about this: days later, as the disciples prayed in the Upper Room, something was shed abroad in their hearts that enabled and even motivated them to go out in love and share the good news of the Gospel in enemy territory. Based on their own feelings, they probably would rather have retaliated! But as God poured out His Spirit on them, His divine compassion superceded their own desires, and they responded as Christ would.

In downtown Columbia, South Carolina, there is a small Church of God with about 150 in attendance on Sunday morning. Not long ago, as they were praying for revival, a homeless man found his way to the church looking for help. Without hesitation, the pastor gave the man some food, some shoes and a place to stay for the night. He helped him contact his family, and miraculously, he even found the man a job. What was amazing, though, was that God supplied the answer to all these needs within hours, something the pastor never could have done on his own. As he sent the man on his way, the pastor told him that if he would come back the following week and bring his friends, he would provide them all with a good meal.

> *To the pastor's surprise, a week later eight homeless people showed up...*

To the pastor's surprise, a week later eight homeless people showed up at the church to eat. Again he fed them, and invited them back the following week. Within several weeks, that little Church of God was feeding over one hundred homeless people on Wednesday nights, and they opened a special worship service for them on Sunday morning at 8:00 a.m. When I visited there, I had the privilege of attending church with about two hundred of the friendliest, happiest street people you would ever want to meet! In fact, the attendance in that early service has exceeded that of their regular worship time.

What touched me about this story was the fact that a small church with limited resources was willing to reach out in love to a group of people who had nothing to offer in return—no suits, no ties, no tithe checks and no social graces. Many of those men and women who had been turned away by society were ushered into the Kingdom by a praying congregation equipped with the Father's compassion.

2. *Urgency*

The second work the Spirit does in us when we pray is fill us with urgency about seeking and saving the lost.

One day the mayor of a small community was driving through the town square area when he noticed two of his own city workers doing something rather unusual. Along one side of the main street, they were working steadily, one of the men digging a hole in the ground, and the other filling it back up. After watching them dig and fill several holes in this manner, the mayor, somewhat confused, confronted the two workers and asked for an explanation. "Well, sir," replied the first man, "we work for the city planting trees, and usually there are three of us — one to dig the hole, one to plant the tree, and one to cover it up. But the guy who plants the tree called in sick today, and," he proudly announced, "we did not want to miss a day's work!"

How easy it is to fall into the habit of just being at church — attend worship, pay our tithe, sing in the choir, attend more services, volunteer some time, give more money, and attend Sunday School. We can become so programmed, that like the tree planters, we totally lose sight of the meaning behind what we are doing. The result is that after years of "doing" church, our relationships are still on the edge, our walk with God is in the same place it has always been, and our lost friends and family members are still without Jesus. We have passed the time, as if just being in the building has been our main objective.

God have mercy on us for just going through the motions! Our mission is one of eternal consequences, and we must never lose a sense of urgency about it. As we pray, the Spirit keeps before us our true purpose. He sets our minds firmly on Kingdom agendas, and instills in us the gravity of what is at stake. Urgency is the adrenaline of those who witness.

In Acts 14:19, we read about how some Jews came from Antioch and Iconium to Lystra and stoned Paul, leaving him for dead outside the city. But after the disciples had gathered around him, instead of escaping, Paul actually "got up and went back into the city." What a crazy thing to do — to go right back into the midst of the very people who tried to kill him. But Paul had an urgency about his message. He knew that the stakes were high, so for the sake of the lost he took chances, risked safety and paid every price.

Our goal is not just to be counted among the regulars on Sunday morning! We are here to make a difference in a dying world. Everything we do should be motivated by the desire to win this generation to Christ, and if we do not have a sense of urgency about that, then we have missed the whole meaning of the cross.

3. Vision

Finally, as we pray, the Holy Spirit gives us a vision for how to win the lost. He will plant a vision for prayer evangelism in anyone who will pray for the Great Commission and sit still long enough to hear His response. I meet people in every part of the country who are absolutely driven by a vision God has given them for their church or city.

Many pastors and leaders I know have a vision for what God wants them to do, and it motivates them past all obstacles and setbacks. They have their eyes set on bigger things than their own salary package or a new building. They are not out to make a name for themselves, but to lift up the name of Jesus over and above their own. However, as they lift up Jesus, people are drawn to them. Every time I talk to one of them they tell me how many people they baptized the previous Sunday, or how many came forward to accept Christ, and how their church is growing. Because they are willing to pray the price, God is using them in dramatic ways.

The Holy Spirit's Work in Unbelievers

1. Convict and Convince

When we begin to ask God to give us the lost people in our cities, the Holy Spirit goes to work in every unbeliever to gently convict them of their sin and convince them of their need for God. Remember, He is the true Evangelist. When we lead someone to salvation, we are only acting as the agent, because the real work has already been done by the Spirit.

> *I believe Jesus intended evangelism to be heart-sell, not hard-sell.*

Although we can not literally see this work going on, it means the difference between success and failure in all of our evangelistic efforts. If we have prayed the price, and are listening to the Father's direction, He will send us on divine appointment to minister to one who is ready to receive. Our opportunity may come over lunch with a client, on the phone with a hurting friend, or in the check-out line at the grocery store. But when God brings together a Christian who is user-friendly and an unbeliever who has been wooed by the Holy Spirit, then evangelism happens almost effortlessly.

I believe Jesus intended evangelism to be heart-sell, not hard-sell. Many people have been hurt by Christians who tried to push them into a commitment without first praying the price, and the result is a frustrating experience for everyone involved. Not only is hard-sell evangelism ineffective, it also tends to drive an unbeliever even further away from the Kingdom.

"No one can say Jesus is Lord except by the Sprit." Jesus Himself said it this way, "No one can come to me unless he is drawn by the Father" (John 6:44). The gentle prodding of the Holy Spirit is the basis of heart-sell. We must realize that unless people see their need for Christ, all the preaching in the world will not make a difference. Unless they feel a heaviness about their sin, it does no good for us to show them the cross. Unless people want to be filled with the presence of Christ, it is no use singing eighteen rounds of "Just As I Am" as they stay just as they are!

2. *Tear Down Walls*

In every city are unseen forces that can hinder people from receiving Christ or can cause them to resist the Gospel. The second thing the Holy Spirit begins to do when we pray is to tear down walls of resistance in the city. For example, in some cities racism and prejudice are so rampant between different people groups that none of the churches can minister effectively until those walls come down. Another unseen force that plays havoc with evangelistic efforts is disunity among believers. How can we demonstrate the love of Jesus to the unchurched when we are too busy criticizing and competing with other believers over secondary issues of the faith? When the church of a city is divided, evangelism will run into all kinds of resistance. Sometimes there are even spiritual forces that need to be disarmed in order to see a breakthrough.

You may be aware of a specific "wall" in your own city that stands in the way of the Great Commission. As you pray through these chapters in Acts, ask God to remove any negative attitudes, feelings, or ideas that may be in the way of your vision. One of the reasons that pastors' prayer summits, citywide concerts of prayer, times of prayer and fasting and other prayer movements have impacted so many cities is that they are springboards for repentance and healing, and they often result in crumbled walls and restoration.

3. Change the Spiritual Climate

Just as every city has a physical climate that affects the temperature, rainfall, humidity, and so forth, they also have a spiritual climate that may determine the fertility for evangelism. Although this concept is difficult to describe, if you have traveled much you know that every city feels a little different. The people are different, attitudes are unique, and priorities may vary. To some degree, the uniqueness of each place is related to spiritual history and receptivity. In other words, some places are more open to the things of God than others!

As you pray, the Holy Spirit will begin to work around you to change the spiritual climate. But you must be persistent. Pray over your spouse and children. Intercede for your city's judicial system, government officials, police and fire departments, public school principals and gangs. Pray over a map of your city or county, targeting your own neighborhood, high crime areas and areas that seem overrun by sin and perversion. Watch for evidence of the Holy Spirit at work to open new doors and make new ways. Be ready for Him to show you creative ideas to reach people you thought were unreachable. Learn to pray for the felt needs of those outside the church, and then watch as the Spirit draws them to your Sunday morning service.

4. Bring People to Jesus

Finally, as you invite the Holy Spirit, you will see people come to Christ and be completed in Him because the Evangelist is at work. The more we come alive in Christ, the more we can offer a life in Him to others. Jesus said, "…open your eyes and look at the fields! They are ripe for harvest" (John 4:35). The end result will be seeing people living in the fullness of Christ for the first time. Christ in us and them is the hope of glory!

How to Use This Guide

Although every chapter in the book of Acts can be prayed over your church and city, I have selected ten chapters—1, 2, 3, 4, 8, 9, 10, 12, 16 and 28—that are especially relevant to what God wants to do today. I believe that as you pray through the selected ten chapters multiple times, the accounts will root deeper and deeper into your own spirit and you will discover the richness of the text as the Holy Spirit leads you through a variety of avenues of intercession. This is known as "index praying"—using the scriptures as an index of prayer ideas.

Acts 29 is designed for you to pray through one chapter a day for ten consecutive days and then start over with Day One, repeating the process until you have prayed through the guide five times. This will equal fifty days, representing the fifty days between Jesus' resurrection and Pentecost. When a group of people will join together in prayer for fifty days, interceding based on these scriptural truths, the Holy Spirit will begin to duplicate what happened in the early church.

The Prayer Guide Format

1. The Word

By way of instruction before you begin to pray, read the passage(s) of scripture for that day to mentally envision the scope of prayer. The additional scriptures will help to reinforce this content. The idea is to creatively voice a prayer based on the Word of God. Whenever possible, use the language of the scriptures. God delights in hearing His Word spoken. As mentioned earlier, it is important to visualize and pray the answer — not the problem. It is crucial to see the need or objective in the light of the Word. Petition with the promises of God in heart and mind and you will come away from your prayer closet much encouraged and uplifted. The Holy Spirit will help you as you pray a Word-based prayer.

> *...visualize and pray the answer — not the problem.*

2. The Needs

The second section of the guide helps you to pray specifically, applying the scripture to needs that you are aware of in your church and city. As you begin, ask the Holy Spirit to bring these needs to mind. Write down names of pastors, leaders, churches, lost people, political leaders, school board members, coaches, etc. As you name them and travail over them in prayer, the Holy Spirit will begin to touch them.

Pray over areas of your city that you normally take for granted such as police departments, hospitals, court systems and schools. Write down numerical goals for baptisms, Sunday School, small groups, financial needs, etc. As you name them, the Holy Spirit will know your heart's desire and He will move accordingly. It is good to write down church goals so you will not forget. If you are a pastor, communicate these to your intercessors. There is great power when the church takes up Kingdom agendas and tenaciously seeks God for their fulfillment.

3. *The Answers*

The final section provides a place for you to write down the answers to prayer. When someone makes a profession of faith — write his or her name down. When someone is healed, write it down. When a goal is reached, write it down. These praise reports serve to encourage you and help to plot your progress in praying. In addition, the Lord is honored and blessed when we give thanks to Him for His mighty works. These testimonies serve as an ongoing reminder of His willingness to answer our prayers.

Practical Ideas to Get Started

1. *Share the vision.*

When you get ready to use *Acts 29*, share the vision first with the church leaders, then find a way to announce the prayer plan from the pulpit. If you are a pastor, you might preach a series on prayer introducing the plan.

2. *Recruit and educate pray-ers*

Have people sign up to pray and sell them this prayer guide. Asking them to pay for the guide helps create a sense of ownership in the journey. Meet with them to explain the guide itself, taking them through Acts, highlighting the works of the Holy Spirit and how they apply to your church's and city's needs. Teach them about the incredible power that lies in corporate prayer. This whole process is an educational effort to bring them on board. The more they understand, the more excited they will become. Keep in mind that if all your church knows is personal prayer, it will take time to establish the new mindset for corporate prayer.

3. Select a coordinator.

If you are a pastor, ask the Spirit to guide you to some-one who can coordinate the prayer journey. This person can keep track of who is praying, answer questions about the prayer guide and help plan meetings at the beginning and end of the journey. He or she might also find a creative way to give feedback to the participants during the time of commit-ment. Meet with the coordinator and plan practical ways to keep the church focused on the *Acts 29* emphasis.

4. Be creative.

The Holy Spirit is very resourceful when it comes to prayer. He will show you creative ways to start using *Acts 29* in your church. Perhaps you could plan a weekend seminar on prayer or take your leadership to visit a praying church. Start a Sunday School class on prayer. Pray through the book of Acts by yourself for a while to really prepare your own heart.

> *Failing to iden-tify the "finish line" is one of the greatest killers of prayer ministries.*

5. Define the time of prayer.

Before you begin, it is important to set a specific starting date and a definite closing date. Defining the time of prayer will help people to maintain an intensity and a commit-ment to pray. Failing to identify the "finish line" is one of the greatest kill-ers of prayer ministries. If people do not know when they can stop praying, they will inevitably give up at some point. This may lead to a sense of failure.

As mentioned before, *Acts 29* was originally designed to start on Pentecost Sunday and last for fifty days. This plan of praying through Acts is ideal to give emphasis to the Holy Spirit during the Pentecost season. Yet, it is also ideal as a guide for Lenten prayer or leading up to an important event such as a revival or special outreach. *Acts 29* could even be prayed throughout the whole year using seven different groups of intercessors.

6. *Give the prayer team a name.*

Giving the prayer team a name will enable participants to identify with an esteemed group in the church. This will facilitate a sense of unity and camaraderie. If possible, have one of the team members report on an answer to prayer at every worship service. If you are a pastor, commend the prayers often and encourage others to join in.

7. *Be open to the Spirit.*

Scripture praying is like priming a pump and it will likely cause a river of ideas to begin to flow. Use other chapters if necessary. Pray with a partner or in small groups of three or four. Be open to creative ways in which the prayer guide might be used. You could use the guide as a format for a 24-hour prayer chain or an all night prayer vigil. A college group or youth group could pray through *Acts 29* targeting the public schools in your area. As an individual, you could pray *Acts 29* over your family or workplace. It is an excellent personal prayer challenge to incorporate into your own devotional time to help you pray more evangelistically.

8. *Be persistent.*

The enemy hates a praying church, and he will do everything he can to diffuse interest and hinder completion of the

Acts 29 prayer journey. But no matter what, press on because you are forming good prayer habits in your church that will carry you to greater victories in the future. Praying churches are not built overnight — be patient.

Seeds need to be planted to reap corporate prayer and the harvest will come in due season.

The enemy hates a praying church.

---

9. *Maintain a spirit of praise.*

The Holy Spirit is a spirit of praise and He loves to dwell and work in the praises of God's people. As you see Acts 29 being written in your city, praise God! Give thanks continually for bold preaching, new converts, and Damascus Road experiences. Praise Him for defeating the enemy, raising up Philips and restoring people to the Body. Putting on the spirit of praise will turbo-charge your prayer efforts.

10. *Appreciate those who pray.*

Following the designated time of prayer, have a fellowship for those who participated and share together what God did. Perhaps you could plan a cookout or potluck dinner. Ask them to share testimonies and insights that they recorded as the Holy Spirit revealed them. This will reinforce the sense of teamwork and help instill a feeling of satisfaction in what was accomplished.

A Word of Personal Encouragement

1. Verbally commit yourself to pray all the way through the journey.

2. Establish a definite time and place to pray.

3. Fight interruptions with a vengeance.

4. Do not be discouraged if you miss a day or two of prayer. Simply pick up where you left off.

5. Ask someone to hold you accountable if possible.

6. Be flexible. This is only a suggested plan of prayer. The Holy Spirit may lead you in another direction to pray.

7. Communicate with others who are praying to compare notes and praise reports. Record the answers for further encouragement.

8. Trust the Holy Spirit and keep before you the urgency of what you are praying about.

The Spirit's Challenge

Right now we are in a prayer epidemic! The Holy Spirit is raising up a great prayer force all across the earth because the Father wants to see whole cities declaring the name of Jesus! Pastors are praying together; denominational and racial walls are being torn down as Kingdom agendas are taking preeminence. Behold, God is doing a new thing and you are taking part in it! (Isaiah 43:18-19).

Day 1

Thy Kingdom Come
Acts 1:1-14

As you pray Acts 1:1-14, think about this — the early church had none of the resources that we have today. They had no family life center, no sanctuary, no office complex, no written curriculum, no formal Sunday School, no seminaries, not even the written Word. They had no budget because they had no money. They had no program directors because they had no programs.

With little education, they were up against almost insurmountable odds. Their society was overrun with pagan cults and national gods, and there were tremendous cultural-ethnic barriers to cross. As a group, they were an odd lot recruited from various walks of life — tax collectors, fishermen, you name it. Their leader had died the death of a criminal. They frequented jails and stirred up riots. They even let women be a part of their ranks, to say nothing of slaves and sinners.

Yet, these believers in Jesus turned the world upside down. With little of what we have today, they spread the Gospel all over the countryside. Why? The Holy Spirit became their foremost resource. He made the difference!

To pray Acts 1 is to invite the Holy Spirit to come and empower us to be His witnesses. The key verse is Acts 1:8, "But you will receive power when the Holy Spirit comes on you; and you

Their leader died the death of a criminal.

will be my witnesses in Jerusalem, and in all Judea and Samaria, and to the ends of the earth." Jesus had just been teaching the disciples about the Kingdom of God (Acts 1:3), and now He was instructing them to go out and tell others. But in order to be His witnesses, they first needed to receive the power of the Holy Spirit. So Jesus told them to wait and pray until the Spirit came.

We read, "They all joined together constantly in prayer, along with the women and Mary the mother of Jesus, and his brothers" (Acts 1:14). They weren't preaching, teaching, singing or planning—they were praying constantly just as Jesus had said. They were convinced of one thing—they dare not go out before they received the power Jesus had told them about!

The Holy Spirit is the true Evangelist.
He spotlights Jesus (John 15:26).
He is our helper in ministry (John 14:15-16, 18, 26).
He is power to embolden ministry (Acts 4:17, 33).
He is the source of abiding fruit (Galatians 5:21).
He convicts and convinces the world (John 16:7-11).
He causes prayer to happen (Romans 8:26).
He works miracles in Jesus' name (Acts 3).
He guides the church in mission (Acts 13:1-3).
He tells us what to say when needed (Mark 13:11).
No wonder the early church did not dare move without this promise from the Father!

Prayer always attracts the Holy Spirit. When Jesus was baptized, "*as he was praying*, Heaven was opened, and the

Holy Spirit descended on him in bodily form like a dove" (Luke 3:21). Later at the scene of the Transfiguration, as Jesus was praying, "the appearance of his face changed, and his clothes became as bright as a flash of lightning" (Luke 9:29). As we pray, so shall we receive the Holy Spirit.

Pray as in Acts 1:14. Ask Jesus to fill your church, your pastor, and your leaders with the Holy Spirit. He said, "If you then, though you are evil, know how to give good gifts to your children, how much more will your Father in heaven give the Holy Spirit to those who ask him?" (Luke 11:13).

The Word

PONDER Acts 1:1-14 and let the Holy Spirit guide in prayer using these scriptures for local application:

"After His suffering, he showed himself to these men and gave many convincing proofs that he was alive. He appeared to them over a period of forty days and spoke about the Kingdom of God" (Acts 1:3).

"But you will receive power when the Holy Spirit comes on you, and you will be my witnesses in Jerusalem, and in all Judea and Samaria and to the ends of the earth" (Acts 1:8).

"When the Counselor comes, whom I will send to you from the Father, the Spirit of truth who goes out from the Father, he will testify about me; but you also must testify, for you have been with me from the beginning" (John 15:26-27).

"You did not choose me, but I chose you and appointed you to go and bear fruit—fruit that will last. Then the father will give you whatever you ask in my name. This is my command: Love each other. If the world hates you, keep in mind that it hated me first" (John 15:16-18).

The Needs

BESEECH Jesus to bless your denominational leaders with a strong understanding of the Kingdom of God (Acts 1:3). List them by name:

1.

2.

3.

4.

5.

ASK Jesus to fill your pastor and local leadership with the Holy Spirit (Acts 1:8). Include Bible teachers (II Peter 1:21).

"...But men moved by the Holy Spirit spoke from God." (RSV)

ENTREAT Jesus to loosen a spirit of corporate prayer in your church (Acts 1:14). Ask Him to...

raise up intercessors

add prayer groups

renew the current prayer ministries

make your church a House of Prayer (Matthew 21:13)

IMPLORE The Holy Spirit to anoint the following ministries, naming their leaders:

Children's Ministries

Evangelism

Missions

Sunday School

Worship

AMEN By praying these promises

"In that day you will no longer ask me any-thing. I tell you the truth, my Father will give you whatever you ask in my Name" (John 16:23).

"You did not choose me, but I chose you and appointed you to go and bear fruit—fruit that will last. Then the Father will give you any-thing you ask in my name" (John 15:16).

The Answers

Record answers and insights giving thanks to God:

"Let them give thanks to the Lord for his unfailing love and his wonderful deeds for men" (Psalm 107:15).

DAY 2

Apostolic Preaching
Acts 2

On the day of Pentecost, Peter preached a powerful message. His preaching was characteristic of the kind of preaching we find in the book of Acts. If we are to see Acts 29 in our cities, we need this bold apostolic preaching.

Consider these marks of apostolic preaching and pray that they will be evidenced in our pulpits today:

1. Jesus was preached as the fulfillment of Old Testament prophecy. Peter refers to Joel 2:28-32 and Psalm 16:8-11 as he proclaims Jesus to his hearers.

2. Jesus was preached as the only Savior. His cross is mentioned as the only hope for the forgiveness of sins (Acts 2:23-24).

3. Jesus is preached as a risen Lord. Apostolic preaching tells of Jesus who died, was raised and is here and now (Acts 2:29-32).

4. Jesus is affirmed as the final authority for all mankind

(Acts 2:33). Peter says, "Therefore let all Israel be assured of this: God has made this Jesus, whom you crucified, both Lord and Christ" (Acts 2:36).

5. Jesus is preached as the standard of righteousness and holiness by which all men must repent and be baptized (Acts 2:38).

6. Jesus is also preached as the Baptizer in the Holy Spirit. Spiritual fullness follows apostolic preaching (Acts 2:38b-39).

7. Jesus is preached as having been attested to by signs and wonders (Acts 2:22).

8. **Those who accepted the message were baptized, and about three thousand were added to their number that day" (Acts 2:41).**

We pray over Acts 2 because of our need today for this kind of anointed, bold preaching in our pulpits. Religious homilies will not budge people out of their complacency. Business as usual on Sunday morning will not strengthen families or impact racial tensions. Passionless preaching produces nothing more than apathetic compliance in the pews.

> *Religious homilies will not budge people out of their complacency.*

Furthermore, Acts 2:42-47 provides a model for discipleship and fellowship among believers. New converts did not just fill out decision cards—they devoted themselves to apostolic teaching, to fellowship, to the breaking of bread, and to prayer. We pray based on these scriptures that the same community life will happen in our churches. No matter the size of your church these truths are applicable to express New Testament Christianity. As they met in homes (Acts 2:46), Jesus became real to them in a new and profound love for each other.

Ask the Holy Spirit to give us men and women who fear only God and hate sin and will preach with a passion for souls. Beseech the Holy Spirit to cleanse us of gimmicks, catering to church visitors, conversion without repentance, apathy to the supernatural, and all attempts to water down the Gospel. Pray for strong Christ-centered, Bible-soaked messages that call for disciples, not just decisions. Yearn for preaching that confronts sin and compassionately calls men to Christ. Invite the Holy Spirit to multiply small groups in your church. Envision supernatural breakthroughs in untouched areas of your community. Read Acts 2 with zeal to pray for a fresh breeze of the Holy Spirit.

The Word

ESTEEM Acts 2 and pray specifically using these scriptures and any others:

> *"We hear them declaring the wonders of God in our own tongues!" (Acts 2:11).*

> *"In the last days, God says, I will pour out my spirit on all people" (Acts 2:17).*

> *"Therefore let all Israel be assured of this: God has made this Jesus, whom you crucified, both Lord and Christ" (Acts 2:36).*

> *"We proclaim Him, admonishing and teaching everyone with all wisdom, so that we may present everyone perfect in Christ" (Colossians 1:28).*

The Needs

SUPPLICATE the Holy Spirit to cause many in your city to extol the wonders of God (Acts 2:11). Name specific neighborhoods, schools, organizations, etc. Pray on site if possible.

PETITION that Jesus be lifted up in your pastor's message and in the praise time (Colossians 1: 28).

CLAIM apostolic results of repentance and water baptism (Acts 2:37-38).

Name the following in prayer:

1.

2.

3.

4.

5.

"No one can come to me unless the Father who sent me draws him ..." (John 6:44).

ENVISION the multiplying of small groups in your church as in Acts 2:42. Pray for an exact number of _____.

Welcome the presence of signs and wonders in Acts 2:43. Request that specific troubled homes be healed and exemplify Acts 2:46.

INVITE the Holy Spirit to add to your number daily those who are being saved (Acts 2:47, 5:14, 9:42, 11:21).

AMEN by extolling God for the gift of His son: "Thanks be to God for his indescribable gift" (II Corinthians 9:15).

The Answers

Note these answers and revelations:

"And they were all amazed at the greatness of God" (Luke 9:43).

DAY 3

Boldness in Jesus' Name
Acts 3

Acts 3 tells the story of a paralytic who was healed at the Gate Beautiful when Peter and John prayed for him. He had been begging there at the Gate for many years, but on that day, he received a gift much more precious than gold or silver. The significant thing about this miracle, however, was the glory that it brought to the name of Jesus.

Acts 4:10 states, "It is by the Name of Jesus Christ of Nazareth, whom you crucified but whom God raised from the dead, that this man stands before you completely healed." He adds in verse 12, "Salvation is found in no one else, for there is no other name under heaven given to men by which we must be saved." Since everyone in that city had probably seen the paralytic before, his testimony as he went running and leaping through town was very powerful! Jesus was exalted through his healing.

Pray in Acts 3 that the name of Jesus will be glorified in your church, especially through the evidence of changed lives. Pray that His power will be displayed for all to see, and that

His name will be exalted above our various titles and self-proclamations. He is to be lifted up over church and denominational labels, names of pride and self-importance. If we are to see the book of Acts rewritten today—healing, salvation, deliverance—it will be done in the power of His name.

It is important to note that when Peter and John prayed for the paralytic, they prayed "in Jesus' name." This is critical for several reasons:

1. In the Old Testament, each time God gave His name, He revealed something about Himself. Now, the nature of God is revealed in one name—Jesus. When we pray in His name we ask only those things that are within the scope of His character.

2. In Jesus' name we have access to the throne of God. Jesus said, "...I tell you the truth, my Father will give you whatever you ask in my name" (John 16:23). We bring petitions before the Father based on Jesus' righteousness, not ours (1 John 5:14-15).

3. The goal of prayer is to know God intimately, and in Jesus' name we have a bond of oneness. Like in all covenant relationships, Jesus gave His name as a symbol of our standing with His Father (John 17:6).

> *When you pray in Jesus' name, you are saying, "I was bought with a price and I am His."*

4. In Jesus' name we have Kingdom authority. "He called his twelve disciples to him and gave them authority to drive out evil spirits and to heal every disease and sickness"(Matthew 10:1). This authority is exercised in the name of Jesus.

5. In Jesus' name ownership is fixed. When you pray in Jesus' name, you are saying, "I was bought with a price and I am His. I know He will meet my need because He takes care of His own."

6. In Jesus' name we are protected from the evil one. Since all power in heaven and earth is invested in His name, and all spirits recognize the irrevocable truth of His authority, when we pray in the name of Jesus we are covered (John 17:11-12).

7. In Jesus' name we are given a new nature. When we are born again, we are changed and our new nature is signified by a new name—His name. As we pray we are reminded of our new nature and we aspire to the holiness it warrants.

8. In Jesus' name we bear the reputation of His Kingdom and love. To pray in His name is to protect His glory and holiness in the earth. As we conclude our prayers we often pray, "For His name sake" (Isaiah 63:12, 14, Jeremiah 32:20, Nehemiah 9:10). In other words, "Lord let nothing be done that will bring shame or reproach to your name." People are not saved to bear our name, but His alone!

In Acts 4:18, the religious leaders commanded the disciples not to preach or teach in the name of Jesus because they recognized the power it held. Through it, the Gospel was advanced all over the land. Likewise, if we are to see breakthroughs today, it will be as the church corporately prays His name.

The Word

CONSIDER Acts 3:1-21 and these scriptures as you pray:

"Then Peter said, 'Silver or gold I do not have, but what I have I give you. In the Name of Jesus Christ of Nazareth, walk'" (Acts 3:6).

" I tell you the truth, anyone who has faith in me will do what I have been doing. He will do even greater things than these, because I am going to the Father. And I will do whatever you ask in my Name, so that the Son may bring glory to the Father. You may ask for anything in my Name, and I will do it" (John 14:12-14).

"When you enter a town ... heal the sick who are there and tell them, 'The kingdom of God is near you'" (Luke 10:8-9).

The Needs

PRAY In Jesus' name for the following people to be healed (Acts 3:16):

1.

2.

3.

4.

5.

Lift in prayer these Christian counselors (John 15:26):

1.

2.

3.

PRAISE His name for signs and wonders in the following public schools (Mark 16:20):

1.

2.

3.

4.

5.

LISTEN for a manner to pray over these city officials and governments (I Timothy 2:1-4, Acts 3:19):

1.

2.

3.

4.

5.

AMEN by declaring the majesty of His name and the miracles He has wrought (Psalm 8:1, 9).

Close with this prayer:

"Sovereign Lord, you have made the heavens and earth by your great power and outstretched arm. Nothing is too hard for you. You show love to thousands but bring the punishment for the fathers' sins into the laps of their children after them. O great and powerful God whose name is the Lord Almighty, great are your purposes and mighty are your deeds. Your eyes are open to all the ways of men; you reward everyone according to his conduct and as his deeds deserve. You performed miraculous signs and wonders in Egypt and have continued them to this day, both in Israel and among all mankind, and have gained the renown that is still yours" (Jeremiah 32:17-20).

The Answers

Register His deeds:

"Salvation is found in no one else,
for there is no other Name under heaven given to men
by which we must be saved" (Acts 4:12).

DAY 4

Deliver Us From Evil
Acts 4

In praying and writing *Acts 29*, it is important to realize there is always opposition to vital Christianity. Praying Acts 4 brings a church into this reality. The early church was told to stop preaching or teaching in Jesus' name. The church leaders were put in jail and an attempt was made to stop this movement. But the disciples would not quit. Their answer to the threats was to form a prayer meeting (Acts 4:23-24) and lift their voices to God. They were filled with boldness to go back and do again the very things that had stirred the resistance.

In order to claim a community for Christ, we must overcome these forces that resist the Gospel. I call these oppositional forces strongholds—systems of thinking, attitudes, beliefs and expectations that have developed over time. Strongholds are the citadels of control over a city or area. The business of spiritual warfare is to dismantle the evil strongholds—those established by man—by replacing them with *divine strongholds.* Our primary weapon for accomplishing this is prayer.

As I have traveled all across the nation, I have identified six strongholds that work to oppose the Holy Spirit's movement in a city. In each case, there is a specific prayer emphasis that, if applied with enough persistence, will yield a *divine stronghold* — a system of attitudes, beliefs and expectations that allows God's continual rule and reign in a territory.

1. The stronghold of RELIGION relates to the worship of traditions and doctrines of men, pagan religions, the man-centered gospel, and nominal, "for-the-sake-of-appearance" Christianity. This stronghold is dismantled through the prayer of SEEKING — yearning to see God's face and not just His hand. As we earnestly seek after God with all our hearts, He establishes a divine stronghold of His MANIFEST PRESENCE.

> *Strongholds are the citadels of control over an area.*

2. The stronghold of PRIDE stems from our feelings of independence and self-sufficiency. We rely on our location, our educational degrees, our experience or our innovative programs to draw people into relationship with Christ. But when we pray in BROKENNESS before God, recognizing that we are nothing apart from Him, then He plants His stronghold of SALVATION in our church.

3. The stronghold of ACCUSATION relates mainly to our treatment of pastors and leaders in the Body of Christ. God takes it personally when one He has called is abused or taken for granted. The prayer of HONOR — when we pray protection and blessing over our shepherds — crumbles this stronghold and invites the FAVOR of God to dwell in its place.

4. The stronghold of PREJUDICE is built on attitudes of denominational superiority when we set ourselves above others in the Body of Christ. But where there is unity through the prayer of AGREEMENT, God pours out His BLESSING and the stage can be set for revival.

5. The stronghold of JUDGMENT is felt where self-righteous Christianity sets the spiritual standards based on performance or "works." But as we pray the prayer of COMPASSION, the GRACE of God flows, soothing the wounds of criticism and rejection.

6. The stronghold of FEAR arises out of the issue of control. Political powers, ungodly people, Satan and his principalities and world systems all oppose the movement of the Spirit because they are afraid of losing control over people and situations. The prayer of FAITH dispels fear, and invites God to establish His stronghold of PEACE.

Acts 4 is a call to serve an eviction notice to the forces of evil that dwell in a city and pray in the *divine strongholds* of God. By definition, a stronghold of any kind takes time to develop and is subsequently difficult to take down. But once a *divine stronghold* is established, the Holy Spirit can begin to dwell in a place and produce fruit for the Kingdom.

The Word

REFLECT on Acts 4 and pray specifically with these scriptures in your heart:

"Remember the words I spoke to you: 'No servant is greater than his master.' If they persecuted me, they will persecute you also" (John 15:20).

"But the Lord is faithful, and He will strengthen and protect you from the evil one" (II Thessalonians 3:3).

"Now, Lord, consider their threats and enable your servants to speak your word with great boldness. Stretch out your hand to heal and perform miraculous signs and wonders through the name of your holy servant Jesus" (Acts 4:29-30).

"All the believers were one in heart and mind" (Acts 4:32).

The Needs

BIND in Jesus' name the powers of darkness resisting the Gospel (Matthew 18:18-19). Pray that man's strongholds will be displaced by God's divine strongholds of His manifest presence, salvation, favor, blessing, grace and peace. Hold on to Psalm 90:17.

Pray a prayer of seeking...

Pray a prayer of brokenness...

Pray a prayer of honor...

Pray a prayer of agreement...

Pray a prayer of compassion...

Pray a prayer of faith...

REBUKE distractions as in Acts 6:4.

REQUEST Holy Spirit boldness for your pastor and church leaders (Acts 4:31, I Thessalonians 5:19) for decisions, preaching, confronting issues such as prejudice and economic oppression. Seek courage for leaders to face criticism and doubts.

CONSIDER these verses in behalf of the spiritual leaders in your community:

Colossians 4:2

Luke 18:1

I Corinthians 15:58

Galatians 6:9-10

"Wait for the Lord; be strong, and take heart and wait for the Lord" (Psalm 27:14).

THANK God for His power in giving our testimony to the resurrection of Jesus Christ (Acts 4:33).

The Answers

Praise reports:

"Day after day, in the temple courts and from house to house, they never stopped teaching and proclaiming the good news that Jesus is the Christ" (Acts 5:42).

DAY 5

Evangelistic Outreach
Acts 8

In the book of Acts, one thing is quite evident—those who were ready to tell the good news were constantly finding themselves on divine appointment, at the right place to tell someone who was ready to hear.

In Acts 8, after preaching the good news and baptizing many people in Samaria, Philip heard a strange word from the Lord—go stand on a road outside of town. God did not tell Philip why he was to "go south to the road," nor did He tell him what to do when he got there. He simply said, "Go." But that was not all. As Philip made his way on the road, he met a chariot, and the Spirit nudged him again to go "stay near it." I can just imagine Philip, wandering down this desert road trying to act natural as he thought, "How can I explain this to the chariot driver?"

What Philip may not have realized, however, was that God was orchestrating a divine intersection. He was moving Philip into a specific place in response to an "open window."

After many years of pastoring and sharing the Gospel

under all kinds of circumstances, I have come to the conclusion that every person has a kind of "spiritual window" through which they can receive the message of Jesus. At any given point in time, most people around us are so busy going about their routines that their windows are either shut or only partially open. Life is going smoothly enough that they are not inclined to want to hear what God has to offer them. Any attempts to witness may seem to bounce off and not be heard.

> *But occasionally, someone gets knocked off center...and suddenly their window flies open.*

But occasionally, someone gets knocked off center—some bad news, a disappointment, a loss, a heartbreak, confusion—and suddenly their window flies open as they search for meaning. At that point, they are a conversion waiting to happen.

Because Philip was in tune with God's voice and willing to obey His instruction, no matter how silly it may have seemed, the Ethiopian eunuch, who was a city leader, immediately accepted the message of the Gospel and was baptized!

As you pray through Acts 8, ask God to raise up Philips in your city who will follow the leading of the Spirit and share the message of Jesus with those who are ready to hear. Pray for divine appointments to be fulfilled for effective evangelism. Ask the Holy Spirit to send laborers into all parts of your community where Jesus is not known.

Ask the Father for divine appointments in the county courthouse, the local hospital, the police and sheriff departments, paid and volunteer departments, as well as industrial areas in a given community. The object is to penetrate unique groupings of people with the Gospel. Also, pray creatively for breakthroughs in various special interest organizations such as a motorcycle club, an arts appreciation league or a single-parent co-op. Include the media outlets in your prayer. List them and pray specifically that they be redeemed for the Kingdom of God to publish good news.

As you pray, expect breakthroughs in low income projects, nursing homes, drug houses, local teenage hangouts, and apartment complexes. Wherever there are people, there needs to be a visible witness for Christ.

Acts 8:8 says, "So there was great joy in that city." Imagine the joy caused by healed marriages, changed lives, lower crime rates and public testimonies about Christ. Acts 8 needs to happen again—right where you are!

The Word

OBSERVE Acts 8 and formulate a prayer based on these scriptures as well:

"Therefore go and make disciples of all nations, baptizing them in the name of the Father and of the Son and of the Holy Spirit, and teaching them to obey everything I have commanded you. And surely I will be with you always, to the very end of the age" (Matthew 28:19-29).

"Then he said to his disciples, 'The harvest is plentiful but the workers are few. Ask the Lord of the harvest therefore, to send out workers into his harvest field'" (Matthew 9:37-38).

"Those who had been scattered preached the word wherever they went" (Acts 8:4).

"...the Holy Spirit, ...will teach you all things and will remind you of everything I have said to you" (John 14:26).

The Needs

INTERCEDE that the Gospel will be preached where it has not been heard (Acts 8:4, Matthew 28:19).

BLESS the Lord for raising up "Philips" to evangelize the following areas (Acts 8:5-7):

Court systems

Medical complexes

Police/Fire departments

Industrial areas

REDEEM in prayer the following media groups in your city:

Newspapers

Radio

Television

SEEK God for the following leaders in local and trans-local governments to be saved (Acts 8:35, II Timothy 1:1-6):

Local

1.

2.

3.

State

1.

2.

3.

Pray for a Christian witness in your state capital and in Washington D.C.

Pray for the President and his staff.

EXPECT breakthroughs for professions of faith in difficult areas such as low income housing projects, apartment units, drug cultures, jails, prisons, nursing homes (II Timothy 4:5).

AMEN

"So there was great joy in that city" (Acts 8:8).

The Answers

Answers to corporate prayer:

"Again, I tell you that if two of you on earth agree about anything you ask for, it will be done for you by my Father in heaven" (Matthew 18:1).

DAY 6

Damascus Road Conversions
Acts 9

Without Acts 9 we would possibly not have the apostle Paul. Breathing murderous threats against Christians, he had been going from house to house arresting them. Then, unexpectedly, he was converted to Christ as he traveled down the Damascus Road. No one preached to him, no one read him the four spiritual laws, and no one invited him to church. He simply got arrested by the Holy Spirit!

What caused Paul, then known as Saul, to experience such a spontaneous, dramatic conversion? I believe the Christians in Damascus knew he was coming and they had been praying fervently for him. I believe the prayers of the saints released the Spirit to miraculously transform Saul through a profound, divine encounter.

We always need to keep in mind that, though God *chooses* to work through us, He is not *bound* to use us to bring people unto Himself. The Holy Spirit, the true Evangelist, can confront, Spirit to spirit, and reveal the Lord of Glory to an unbeliever. And when He does, the experience can be nothing less than life-changing.

In a large group of Christians, usually at least one or two came to Christ much like Paul did — they had a Damascus Road experience. They were going through life minding their own business, when suddenly, without warning, they met the living God. I know one man who had such an encounter while being arrested for drunk driving. Hands cuffed behind him, face down on the hood of his car, he looked up into the night sky and saw Jesus! He was instantly sobered and converted. His life was changed forever.

The book of Acts encourages us to pray specifically for people who are not Christians to have Damascus Road conversions. The Holy Spirit might arrest them in times of crisis, or in times of loneliness. He might confront during times of celebration or success. One could even have a Damascus Road conversion while overhauling an engine or shopping at the mall. God is not restricted by setting or location.

> *Sometimes...those individuals who seem the most determined to reject God are the best candidates...*

This section of the guide provides a place to write down specific names and intercede for them to be miraculously converted. Sometimes, just like in Paul's case, those individuals who seem the most determined to reject God are the best candidates for Damascus Road conversions. God has a wonderful sense of humor.

If Paul could be so profoundly saved, others can be converted in similar fashion. God is no respecter of persons. What He did for Paul, He will do again. Acts 9 is a blueprint for us to follow in finding creative ways to pray for non-believers — especially those antagonistic to the faith. Name the hopelessly lost in prayer and ask God to intercept them by the Holy Spirit.

The book of Acts is about church growth and expansion. Lives are changed by Jesus Christ and the Word spreads. Praying in Acts 9 also includes praying for workers like Ananias and Barnabas to be raised up by the Holy Spirit to disciple others in your city. New converts must be discipled in the Word and learn the importance of fellowship as in Acts 2:42.

Ananias prayed for Paul to be filled with the Holy Spirit (Acts 9:17), an infilling that is essential in securing any new believer in the power of God. Trust God to do this again. Unbelievers not only need to find Jesus, but they need to be nurtured so that they will grow in the faith.

Barnabas brought Paul to church (Acts 9:27) and helped him to be accepted by the believers. New converts need this encouragement to become a part of the church. Ask God to raise up such workers as described in Acts 11:23-24. The fruit of Barnabas' ministry is described in this one verse, "...and a great number of people were brought to the Lord." So be it in your city.

The Word

NOTE Acts 9:1-31 and pray these scriptures with specific local application:

"No one can come to me unless the Father who sent me draws him, and I will raise him up at the last day" (John 6:44).

"Therefore I tell you that no one who is speaking by the Spirit of God says, 'Jesus be cursed,' and no one can say, 'Jesus is Lord,' except by the Holy Spirit" (I Corinthians 12:3).

"In the same way, the Spirit helps us in our weakness. We do not know what we ought to pray, but the Spirit himself intercedes for us with groans that words cannot express. And he who searches our hearts knows the mind of the Spirit, because the Spirit intercedes for the saints in accordance with God's will" (Romans 8:26-27).

The Needs

BELIEVE God for the following to have a Damascus Road experience (Acts 1:1-6, Mark 11:23):

1.

2.

3.

4.

5.

TRUST the Father to raise up many like Ananias to go and confirm new converts into the Kingdom (Acts 9:10-19).

Yearn for new converts to be filled with the Holy Spirit (Acts 9:17). Pray that they will have a hunger for the Word.

RAISE up, Lord, a force of men and women like Barnabas to encourage the church to fulfill her mission (Acts 9:26-30).

"When he arrived and saw the evidence of the grace of God, he was glad and encouraged them all to remain true to the Lord with all their hearts. He was a good man, full of the Holy Spirit and faith, and a great number of people were brought to the Lord" (Acts 11:23-24).

SO BE IT in consideration of these pertinent truths:

"This is the assurance we have in approaching God: that if we ask anything according to his will, he hears us ... whatever we ask—we know that we have what we asked of him" (I John 5:14-15).

"The Lord is not slow in keeping his promise, as some understand slowness. He is patient with you, not wanting anyone to perish, but everyone to come to repentance" (I Peter 3:9).

"Endure hardship with us like a good soldier of Christ Jesus. No one serving as a soldier gets involved in civilian affairs—he wants to please his commanding officer" (II Timothy 2:3-4).

The Answers

List new converts and thank God for each of them:

1.

2.

3.

4.

5.

6.

7.

8.

9.

10.

*"Then the church throughout Judea, Galilee and Samaria
enjoyed a time of peace.
It was strengthened; and encouraged by the Holy Spirit,
it grew in numbers, living in the fear of the Lord"* (Acts 9:31).

DAY 7

A Harvest of Households
Acts 10

Acts 10 tells the story of a Gentile named Cornelius, a government official who wanted to know God. He was devout, he gave generously, and he prayed regularly. Yet, he was lost—religious and lost.

Then one afternoon, Cornelius had a vision which frightened him. An angel of the Lord appeared before him and told him that his prayers and gifts to the poor were only a "memorial offering" before God. Suddenly, Cornelius' spiritual window flew open! As he stared at the angel in fear, the angel told him to send for a man named Peter.

As a Jewish man, Peter was forbidden by law to even associate with a Gentile, much less visit his home. But the Lord had also given Peter a vision, releasing him to go and preach the good news to Cornelius and his household. So Peter obeyed God, and went to the home of the Gentile leader.

When Peter shared the news about Jesus, not only was Cornelius saved, but his entire family as well. They all received the Holy Spirit and were baptized that same day.

Seeing an entire family saved was not an unusual thing for the apostles. They often taught and prayed in homes. Ministering to the people in a household was significant in that culture partly because church buildings did not yet exist, and partly because the term "household" referred to the large extended families that typically lived under one roof. When one person received a touch from God, the rest of the family often followed suit and received the Gospel, as in the case of the Roman jailer in Acts 16:29-34.

> *Yet, he was lost — religious and lost.*

Many today are rediscovering the power of ministering to households and families through a ministry called Houses of Prayer Everywhere, or H.O.P.E. All over the country Houses of Prayer are springing up in neighborhoods, workplaces and apartment complexes as a way to evangelize communities. Consider how the apostles worked in the book of Acts:

They broke bread **in their homes** and ate together... (2:46b)

...**from house to house**, they never stopped teaching... (5:42)

The Lord told him, "**Go to the house** of Judas..." (9:11)

"...he **went to the house** of Mary the mother of John..." (12:12)

"...taught you publicly and **from house to house**." (20:20)

As you pray through Acts 10, pray for entire households to be saved. Think about the unchurched households on your street and pray for them by name. Ask God to send families to your church to worship together. Beseech the Holy Spirit to fall on those whose windows might be open on Sunday morning as your pastor preaches (Acts 10:44). Pray also for your church leaders, that they might be always open to where God may want to use them. Pray that their hearts would be turned to the Spirit's voice like Peter's was.

The book of Acts contains story after story of divine appointments like the one in Acts 10. Corporate prayer over Acts 10 yearns for such alignments between those ready to hear and those ready to share: In Acts 3, a cripple is ready to receive healing and salvation; in Acts 8, we see Philip at the right place to give the right message to an Ethiopian who is ripe to hear; in Acts 14:8, a man who was lame suddenly has faith to be healed; in Acts 16:14, Lydia's heart is receptive to the Gospel.

Acts 29 is written when those who are ready are brought face to face with a living witness. These divine encounters in answer to prayer reveal the mystery of God in His sovereign call upon souls. We simply pray, "Lord like the mighty breakthrough to the Gentiles in Acts 10, do it again for all the hungering souls in our community. Amen."

The Word

HEED Acts 10 and pray for an outreach to homes using these scriptures:

"'My food,' said Jesus 'is to do the will of him who sent me and to finish his work. Do you not say, 'Four months more and then the harvest'? I tell you, open your eyes and look at the fields! They are ripe for harvest" (John 4:34-35).

"After this the Lord appointed seventy-two others and sent them two by two ahead of him to every town and place where he was about to go" (Luke 10:1).

"For nothing is impossible with God" (Luke 1:37).

"Therefore confess your sins to each other and pray for each other so that you may be healed. The prayer of a righteous man is powerful and effective" (James 5:16).

The Needs

BOLDLY pray for an alignment between those ready to hear like Cornelius and those ready to tell like Peter (Acts 10:2, 23).

Intercede for these unchurched homes on your street.

1.

2.

3.

4.

5.

Rend, in Jesus' name, the veil of doubt (Matthew 16:19, II Corinthians 4:3-4).

Pray persistently for homes to be healed and saved (Colossians 4:2).

Request for _____ new households per week to visit the church (Hebrews 4:16).

"The word of the Lord spread through the whole region" (Acts 13:49).

DILIGENTLY request ministering homes to reach out to their neighborhoods (Philemon 6) with Bible studies, coffees, fellowships, back yard Bible clubs for kids, etc.

AMEN

"In this way the word of the Lord spread widely and grew in power" (Acts 19:20).

The Answers

Harvest reports:

"Be patient, then, brothers, until the Lord's coming. See how the farmer waits for the land to yield its valuable crop and how patient he is for the autumn and spring rains. You too, be patient and stand firm, because the Lord's coming is near" (James 5:7-8).

DAY 8

Healing Casualties
Acts 12

Since ministry involves relationships between imperfect people, it also involves casualties. Every church could make a list of those who have left their flock hurt or wounded by the words or actions of others. In some cases, the injured leave one church in search of another. Or worse, they simply drop out of fellowship altogether. If we could somehow reclaim all the people who were once part of the Body but have pulled out, hurt by the church or the people in it, I wonder if we would have enough seating to hold them all.

One look at the turnover rate in the pulpits of many of today's churches indicates that casualties among leaders are just as numerous as those within the congregations. Pastoral burn-out is a serious problem. Although all casualties need to be restored to the church, I believe God especially grieves when one of His appointed messengers falls by the wayside due to the pain inflicted by ministry, especially when the tragedy could have been prevented by intentional, focused prayer.

Pastors and spiritual leaders are extremely vulnerable to

attack because they are the point men and women in the spiritual realm. The enemy knows that if he can strike a shepherd, the sheep will scatter, and he loves nothing more than to see an effective spiritual leader fall. Ministry dropouts are always

Ministry dropouts are always painful regardless of the reason.

painful, regardless of the reason. A pastor simply burns out, a leader's marriage falls apart, a youth director is slandered, a Sunday School teacher fails to get recognition, an associate does not receive a much-needed raise — the casualty lists are endless. And the results are the same. Feelings are hurt, a wound is inflicted, they become bound and imprisoned by resentment and anger and ultimately they don't minister any longer.

Our pastors need to be protected and blessed in prayer — we need to build a hedge around them and their families with consistent, loving, faithful intercession. To take them for granted not only works against the effectiveness of the church, but it also dishonors God whom they represent.

In Acts 12, we see that Peter had become a ministry casualty. Herod had arrested him and thrown him in prison, and he intended to have him tried and put to death. But we read in verse 5, "So Peter was kept in prison, but the church was earnestly praying to God for him." Notice that it was not a single church praying for Peter, but *the* church — all the house churches in town. As one voice, they were praying in agreement for his release. The answer — God sent an angel to loosen the chains and set Peter free, restoring him to ministry! What a powerful testimony of prayer for those who are in chains because of wounds inflicted in Kingdom work.

Acts 12 needs to happen again and again in every city so dropouts can be healed and returned to fellowship. Every church needs to see brothers and sisters and even leaders restored. Pray. Name some who have given up on the church and ask God to bring them back. Earnestly request their healing, praying for a spirit of forgiveness to touch all.

Also consider persecuted Christians in other countries that are actually in prison for their faith. Find out who and where so you can pray in an informed manner. As part of the body suffers, we all suffer. When they go free, we are free.

Part of writing Acts 29 means setting captives free through corporate prayer to return them to worship, to prayer, to working in the nursery, to hosting a newcomers' coffee and to filling other vacated positions in the ranks. It means gracefully and prayerfully restoring leaders who have fallen, whatever the reason, into meaningful relationship with the Body. God is greater than any statistics about dropouts. He is greater than any crisis or situation. And He is the Healer, not just of bodies, but of fragmented churches and broken relationships.

The Word

REGARD Acts 12:1-19 and pray today for ministry to casualties and those persecuted for the faith:

"So Peter was kept in prison, but the church was earnestly praying to God for him" (Acts 12:5).

"Suddenly an angel of the Lord appeared and a light shone in the cell. He struck Peter on the side and woke him up. 'Quick, get up!' he said, and the chains fell off Peter's wrists" (Acts 12:7).

"All this I have told you so that you will not go astray. They will put you out of the synagogue; in fact, a time is coming when anyone who kills you will think he is offering a service to God. They will do such things because they have not known the Father or me. I have told you this, so that when the time comes you will remember that I warned you. I did not tell you this at first because I was with you" (John 16:1-4).

The Needs

EARNESTLY request the return of those who no longer attend worship (Acts 12:5, 7, James 5:19-20).

Ask God to heal hurt feelings, confusion, bitterness, pride, discouragement with the church, past wounds, etc.

Beseech Him to send a spirit of forgiveness to permeate the church's committees and business meetings (Ephesians 4:30-32).

REBUKE in Jesus' name the persecution of Christians in the following countries (Colassians 2:1-2, Philippians 1:12).

1.

2.

3.

4.

5.

Enlist God to give the American church a burden for Christians in Africa, Russia, China and other countries known for opposing Christianity.

Appeal to the Holy Spirit for the following missionaries to be protected:

1.

2.

3.

4.

5.

AMEN to Jesus' prayer for unity in the Body of Christ (John 17).

The Answers

Answers and insights from praying in Acts 12:

"And the disciples were filled with joy and with the Holy Spirit"
(Acts 13:52).

DAY 9

Worship Evangelism
Acts 16:16-37

If there is anything that is essential to your church, it is the meaningful, dynamic worship of God. The Spirit of God inhabits the praises of His people, which means that when we lift up praises to the throne, He always comes on the scene. As we worship, the Spirit moves and works in the hearts of those who might be open to receiving Jesus. People may receive healing or a special touch from God. John Wimber says that worshiping God is like inverting a honeycomb of grace—you never know where "gracelets" are going to fall. Acts 16 is a testimony of the power of good worship to draw people into the Kingdom.

With no instruments, no overhead, no hymnals and no music leader, Paul and Silas turned their prison cell into a place of worship. We read, "About midnight Paul and Silas were praying and singing hymns to God, and the other prisoners were listening to them" (Acts 16:25). Imagine, beaten, unjustly handled, humiliated, and uncertain about their future, the two prisoners were singing and praising God.

As a result, the cell was shaken, the door flew open and their chains fell off. This was a pretty powerful worship service! The jailer came in and was so moved by the scene that he asked, "What must I do to be saved?"

I do not believe it was the shaking walls or the clattering of chains falling off that got the jailer's attention. I think the presence of God in that prison was so powerful that it convicted the jailer on the spot, and he was saved along with his whole household.

> *"What must I do to be saved?"*

We could call this "worship evangelism" — no preaching, no teaching, no choir, no invitation, simply two beaten, bruised prisoners lifting up songs of praise to the Lord. But the inspired adoration of God by his children creates a noticeable Holy presence. The act of worship did in that setting what words could not have done, and it will have the same impact today.

Wait on God using this day to pray for your church's worship. Realize you are agreeing with others who are praying *Acts 29* that an excitement and renewal of praise will come to your church — exciting new music, powerful old hymns, special songs unto the Lord, quiet times of waiting on God, serious times of repentance and adoration.

Take the focus of this chapter to church early on Sunday morning and intercede for the worship that day. Ask the Holy Spirit to reveal the presence of God during worship. Ask Him to cause your worship leaders to be sensitive to how the Spirit might be working in the lives of people. Fervently pray for hearts to be stirred and captives to be released. Pray for any special music and speak blessings over the choir or praise team. Perhaps you could anoint the instruments with oil. Envision "gracelets" of physical and emotional healing falling on people throughout the congregation. Invite God to cause people to be saved during worship just as He did the jailer in Acts 16.

Expect high praise as you go to church. Seek Him for exalted worship to take place that will include emotions as well as reason. As you pray for Biblical worship, consider some of the other great prayers of worship and scenes of worship in the Bible like David's adoration in I Chronicles 20:10-13 or II Chronicles 20:1-30.

Rebuke the spirit of entertainment and the religious routines of liturgical drudgery. Bind all the spirits of doubt and apathy to the glory of God. Claim in Jesus' name a hunger for God, a forgetfulness of time, and an uninhibited expression of love for God set in reverence.

The Word

APPLY Acts 16:16-34 in prayer with worship in mind:

"About midnight Paul and Silas were praying and singing hymns to God, and the other prisoners were listening to them" (Acts 16:25).

"Do not get drunk on wine, which leads to debauchery. Instead, be filled with the Spirit. Speak to one another with psalms, hymns and spiritual songs. Sing and make music in your heart to the Lord, always giving thanks to God the Father for everything, in the name of our Lord Jesus Christ" (Ephesians 5:18-20).

"Yet a time is coming and has now come when the true worshipers will worship the Father in spirit and truth, for they are the kind of worshipers the Father seeks" (John 4:23).

The Needs

WAIT on God for wisdom to pray for your church's worship (John 4:23-24).

AGREE in prayer for excitement and renewal of worship and praise (Matthew 18:18).

Request the manifestation of God's presence in the services (Psalm 22:3).

Pray for a spirit of thanksgiving in the musicians and singers (Psalm 100:4).

Beseech the Holy Spirit to anoint your worship leaders.

"So he said to me, 'This is the word of the Lord to Zerubbabel: 'Not by might nor by power, but by my Spirit,' says the Lord Almighty" *(Zechariah 4:6).*

LOOSEN a spirit of conviction for sin and a desire for conversion in your worship services (Acts 16:30-31).

Envision many asking the question: "Sirs, what must I do to be saved?" Bind unbelief and doubt.

AMEN in this prayer with David:

"David praised the Lord in the presence of the whole assembly, saying:

'Praise be to you, O Lord, God of our Father Israel, from everlasting to everlasting. Yours, O Lord, is the greatness and the power and the glory and the majesty and the splendor, for everything in heaven and earth is yours.

Yours, O Lord, is the kingdom; You are exalted as head over all. Wealth and honor come from you; you are the ruler of all things. In your hands are strength and power to exalt and give strength to all. Now, our God, we give you thanks, and praise your glorious name'" (I Chronicles 29:10-13).

The Answers

Record victories in worship:

"So the churches were strengthened in the faith and grew daily in numbers" (Acts 16:5).

DAY 10

Shake and Bake
Acts 28:1-10

Good wants us to complete what we begin for Him. What good is it if we begin the race, and can not finish the course? You can be sure of this one thing, as you begin to light a revival fire by praying through the book of Acts, the vipers of the enemy will come out to strike you and even stop you. Satan hates the supernatural works of Jesus in the church. He will lash out with venomous lies, destructive gossip and the opinions of men in order to poison the ranks and cause internal strife.

So how did the apostles handle these attacks of the enemy? Notice in Acts 28 that as Paul was building a fire, a viper jumped out from the flames and latched onto his hand. The natives, recognizing the snake as poisonous, expected Paul to die. But to their surprise, Paul shook the viper into the fire and was unharmed.

As you pray through Acts 28, pray for steadfastness according to Paul's example:

1. He ignored the viper. He did not talk about it or seek sympathy from others. He gave it no undue attention. If the devil can not stop you, he at least wants your attention and he will go to any extreme to get you to focus on the "vipers." Instead of giving in to his schemes, enter into a time of praise. Praise God for past victories, for His promises, and for the armor of God in Ephesians 6.

2. Paul shook the viper off. Do something to shake off the attack. Pray that the church as a whole will learn how to overcome the evil one together. Call a special prayer vigil, sow a tape or book on spiritual warfare, enlist some to pray and fast for a season. Learn what others are doing to shake off attacks and copy their strategy.

3. Since the fire represents the Holy Spirit, after you shake, you need to "bake." Put the viper in the fire, submitting it under authority of the name of Jesus. Pray for discernment about the spiritual nature of the onslaught and petition God for wisdom and strategy. The Holy Spirit is a good helper and counselor. When the enemy comes in like a flood, rise and seek the Spirit's guidance. He has the answer to every scheme of the devil because He has seen them all. He will tell you what to do and what not to do. He will instruct you and guide you. He will also tell you when to simply rest.

4. Paul continued to minister right after the attack. He prayed for the publican's father who was healed and this opened the door for others to come and be cured. Note — the enemy sent a snake to stop Paul, but he shook it off and ended up praying for the sick on the island. What began as an assignment of death was turned into an instrument of revival. Ask God for this kind of wisdom and maturity to enable you to divert the devil's plans and use them to further the Gospel.

> *What began as an assignment of death was turned into an instrument of revival.*

Imagine what kind of opportunities might be created if we could learn how to use "the vipers" as catalysts for revival instead of allowing them to make us retreat into bunkers of self-preservation.

Paul knew about riots, mobs, false accusations, deceitful brothers, stonings, lions, and other dangers. The enemy threw everything at Paul to stop him, but eventually he would write, "… the time has come for my departure. I have fought the good fight, I have finished the race, I have kept the faith" (II Timothy 4:7). Would that we could finish our course and not give up!

Watch in a discerning manner for any surprise assaults from the enemy. Trust God for the victory no matter what you may hear or feel. Remember the battle is the Lord's and the victory is yours in Him.

The Word

MEDITATE on Acts 28:1-10 and pray these scriptures for victory and steadfastness in your church's mission:

"But Paul shook the snake off into the fire and suffered no ill effects" (Acts 28:5).

"'... no weapon forged against you will prevail, and you will refute every tongue that accuses you. This is the heritage of the servants of the Lord, and this is their vindication from me,' declares the Lord" (Isaiah 54:17).

"Therefore, my dear brothers, stand firm. Let nothing move you. Always give yourselves fully to the work of the Lord, because you know that your labor in the Lord is not in vain" (I Corinthians 15:58).

The Needs

RESIST in Jesus' name attacks on your pastor and church leadership (Acts 20:28-31). Stand against power struggles.

BUILD a hedge of protection around your church's finances (Job 2:10, Ephesians 6:10-20).

Stand in prayer, girded in truth (Ephesians 6:14).

Meditate the merits of Jesus Christ (Ephesians 6:14).

Receive the peace of Jesus on behalf of your men's and women's groups (Ephesians 6:15).

Cover your teens and youth workers with the shield of faith, quenching darts of peer pressure (Ephesians 6:16).

Take the helmet of salvation to cancel effects of ungodly advertisement and music (Ephesians 6:17).

Assert in prayer the power of the Word against vain imaginations (Ephesians 6:17).

"And pray in the Spirit on all occasions with all kinds of prayers and requests. With this in mind, be alert and always keep on praying for all the saints" (Ephesians 6:18).

WATCH and pray for a discerning manner to guard the overall ministries of the church (Mark 13:33, 37).

AMEN as you pray in the light of Romans 8:28 so that in all things God is glorified in your church (Acts 28:7-10).

"They will lift you up in their hands, so that you will not strike your foot against a stone" (Psalm 91:12).

"The Lord is with me; I will not be afraid. What can man do to me?" (Psalm 118:6).

The Answers

Notes and reflections:

"...no weapon forged against you will prevail, and you will refute every tongue that accuses you" (Isaiah 54:17a).

Finally...

    EXPECT God to do again what He did in the book of Acts in your church and community (Ephesians 3:20-21).

    CONFESS the work of the Holy Spirit to bring to reality the Kingdom of God in every area of your community.

    ENCOURAGE one another as you pray together in this ministry (Hebrews 10:25).

    CONTINUE to pray through the book of Acts in your daily devotional time. As an added challenge, read one chapter a day corresponding to the date (read chapter one on the first of each month, chapter two on the second, etc.) praying each chapter over your church, your neighborhood and your family.

    "Then the church throughout Judea, Galilee and Samaria enjoyed a time of peace. It was strengthened; and encouraged by the Holy Spirit, it grew in numbers, living in the fear of the Lord" (Acts 9:31).